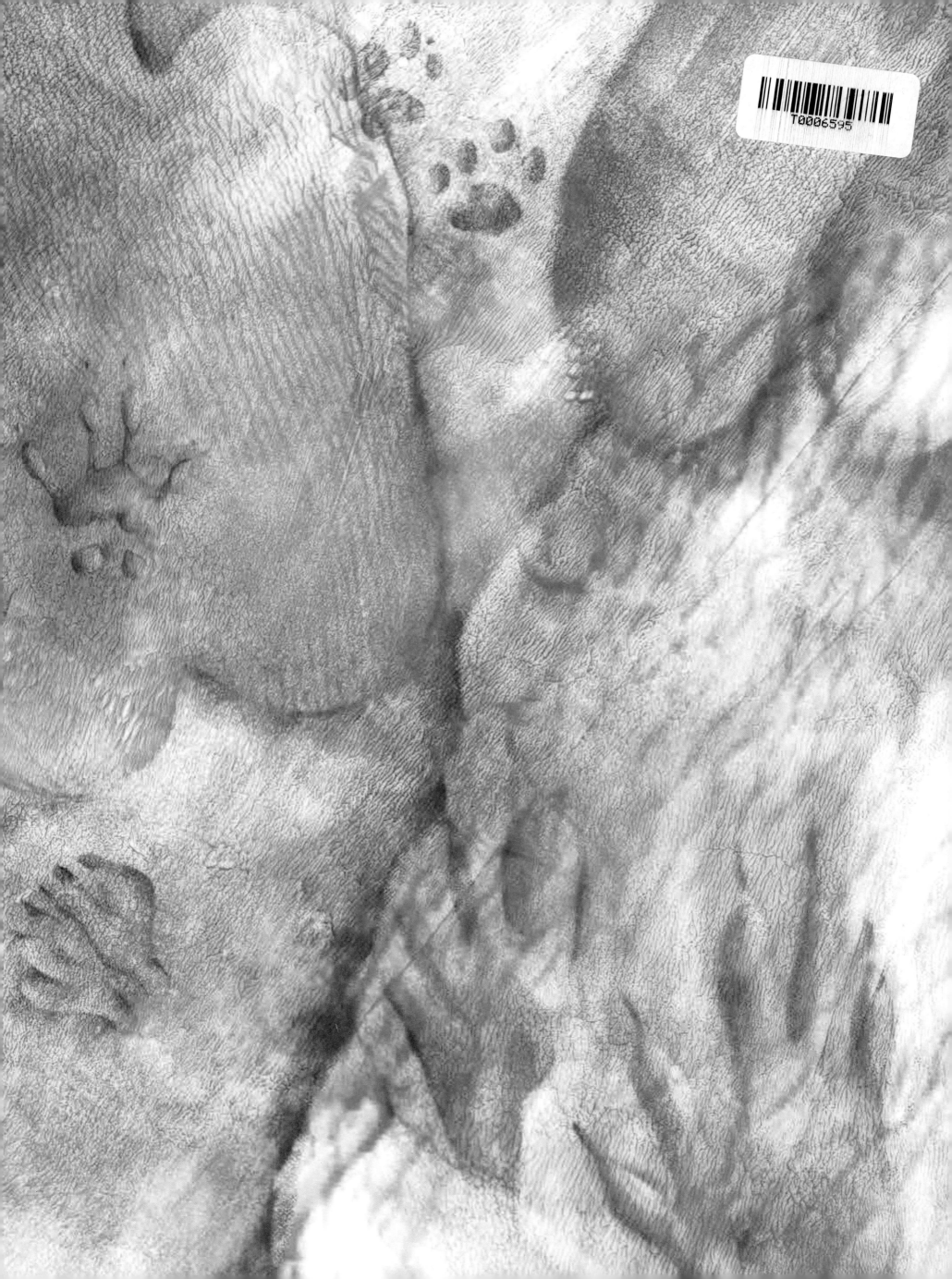

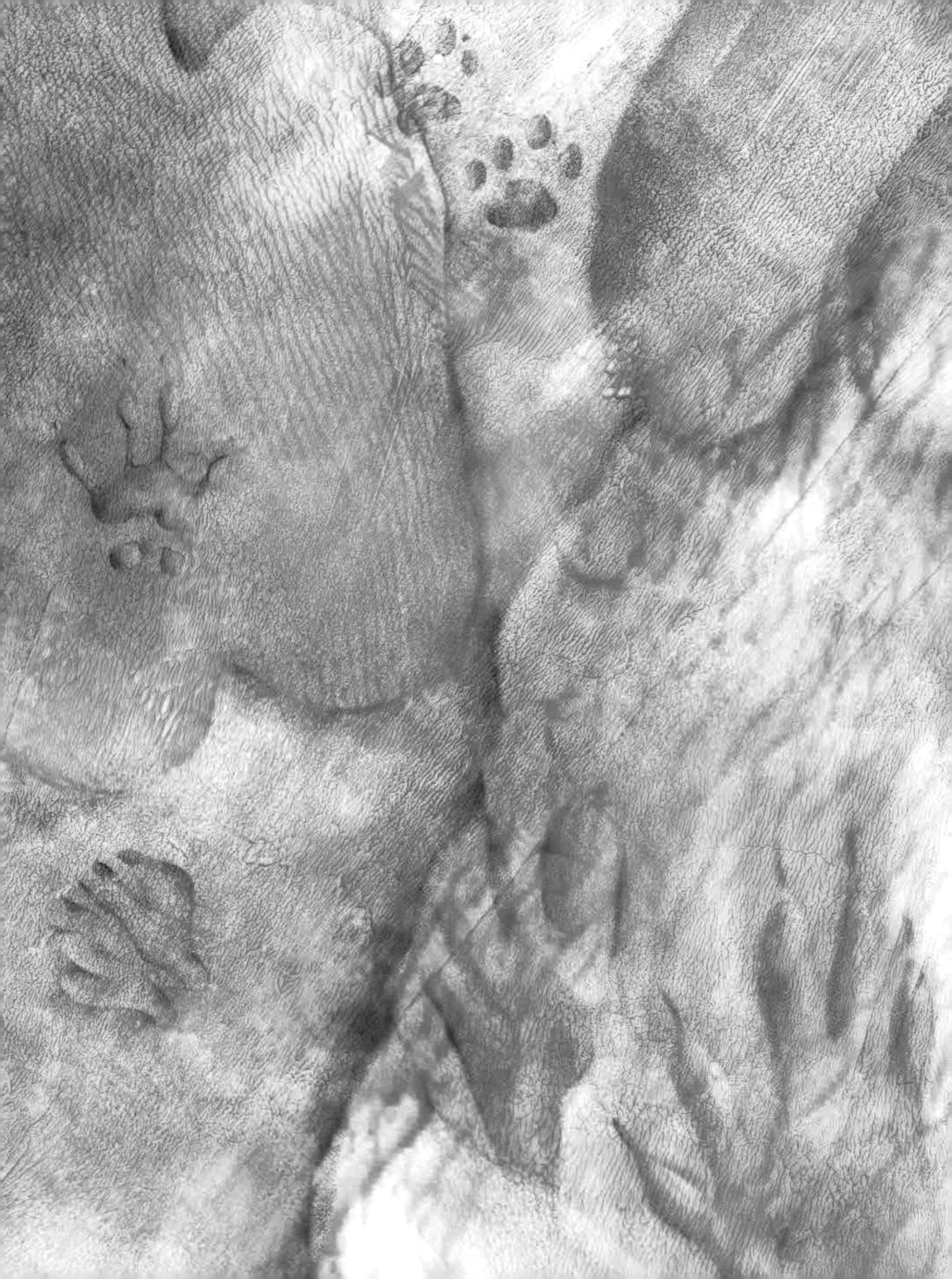

LIFE-SIZE ANIMALS

AN ILLUSTRATED SAFARI

written by
RITA MABEL SCHIAVO

illustrated by
ISABELLA GROTT

Abrams Books for Young Readers
New York

CONTENTS

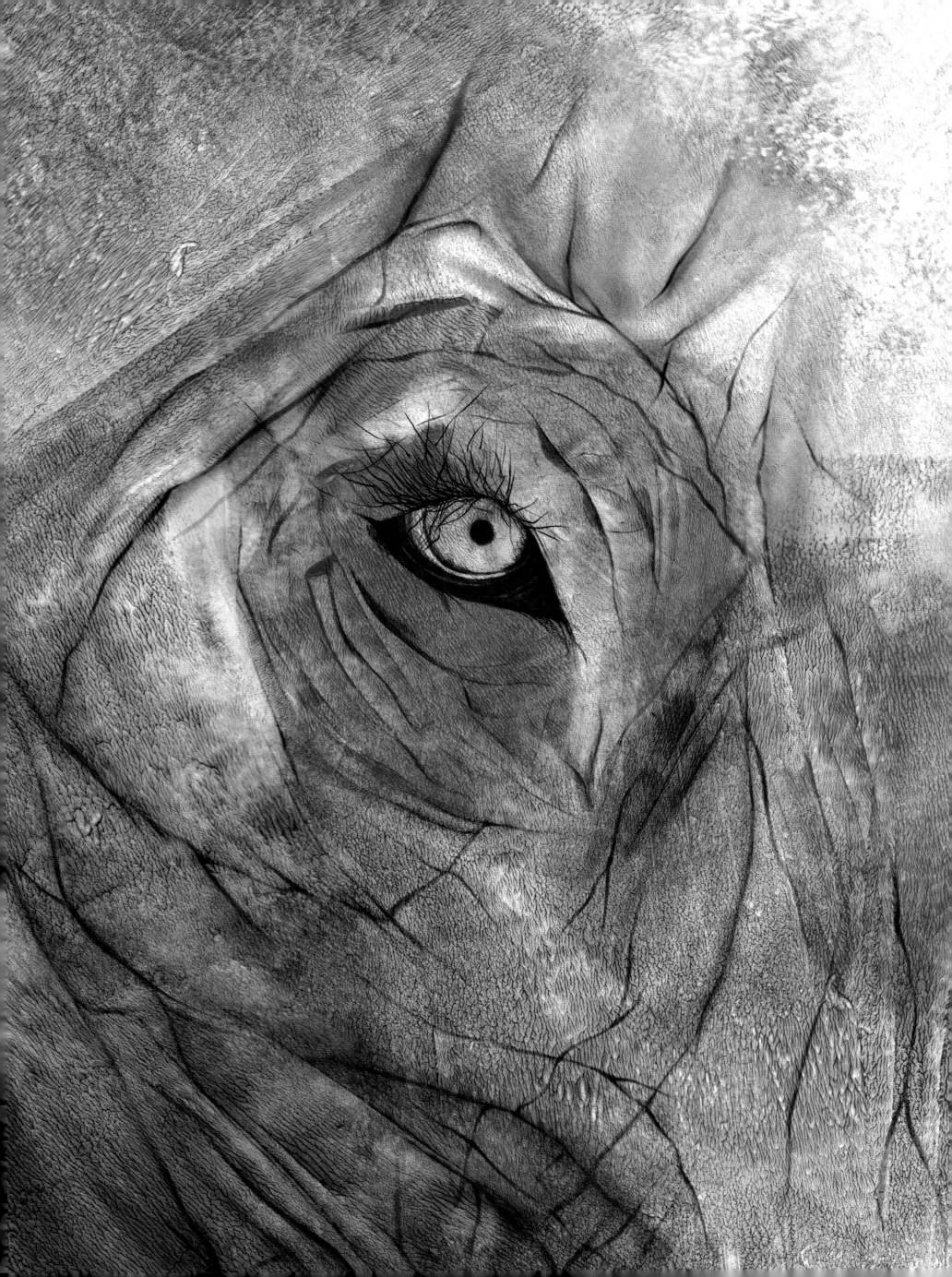

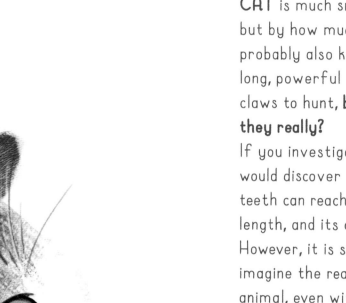

Everybody knows that the domestic **CAT** is much smaller than a **TIGER,** but by how much, exactly? You probably also know that a tiger has long, powerful fangs and uses strong claws to hunt, **but how big ARE they really?**
If you investigated a little bit, you would discover that a tiger's canine teeth can reach up to 4 inches in length, and its claws exceed 4 inches. However, it is still difficult to imagine the real size of this animal, even with a ruler.

This book helps you to get to know what animals are really like using **accurate illustrations that have the actual measurements beside them.**
Flipping through the pages, you can begin to imagine meeting the smallest or largest members of the animal kingdom, from insects to whales, and compare their eggs, tusks, tongues, tails, footprints, and eyes. At the same time, you'll learn all about these animals.

Did you know, for example, that a little chameleon has a tongue that is twice as long as its body? And do you know how big a giant spider is? Did you know that a blue whale's eye is tiny when compared to its immense body?

Dive into the animal world and look at it from this unique perspective!

WARRIORS OF THE SUN

The hummingbird family is filled with some of the smallest and most unusual birds. Hummingbirds can beat their wings up to **80 times per second**, hover in the air, stay in place, and fly backwards! They feed mainly on nectar, supplementing their diet with insects to have enough energy. The smallest ones in the group are the **bee hummingbird (Helena hummingbird)** and the **vervain hummingbird.** They weigh less than **1 ounce**, and the females can grow up to **2.75 inches** in length.

VERVAIN HUMMINGBIRD—LENGTH 2.75 IN

GIRAFFE—OVER 19.7 IN

The **Malayan sun bear** has an omnivorous diet and a long tongue, useful for catching insects inside the cracks of tree trunks.

A **giraffe**'s purple tongue is able to easily tear off acacia leaves without getting pricked by the huge thorns.

MALAYAN SUN BEAR—UP TO 10 IN

The **okapi** uses its dark purple tongue to clean its nose and ears.

One of the smallest species of chameleon, the **rosette-nosed chameleon** (*Rampholeon spinosus*) has a tongue two and a half times its body length and can speed up much more quickly than those of larger species.

ROSETTE-NOSED CHAMELEON—5 IN

OKAPI—ABOUT 18 IN

A **woodpecker**'s tongue can reach the same length as its body. It's so long that it can't be contained inside its mouth and remains rolled up inside a special channel, which starts from the beak and goes back into the head, around the skull, and returns to the beak on the opposite side.

GIANT ANTEATER—2 FT

WOODPECKER—UP TO 6 IN

To eat up to 35,000 ants and termites a day, the toothless **giant anteater**, uses its tongue, which is by far the longest of any animal in the animal kingdom.

The small **tube-lipped nectar bat** (*Anoura fistulata*) rarely reaches 2.5 inches in length and has a tongue longer than its body, which it uses to feed mainly on nectar.

TUBE-LIPPED NECTAR BAT — 3.5 IN

SIBERIAN TIGER—4 IN

AFRICAN LION—3.5 IN

The Siberian tiger is the largest of all of the felines! It can weigh more than 660 pounds, which is enough weight to kill a deer in a single bound. Its claws can unsheath and are very sharp.

The African lion is the king of the Savannah. It possesses robust claws that are the perfect weapons for grabbing and holding on to its prey.

HARPY EAGLE—5 IN

GOLDEN EAGLE—2.6 IN

This large bird of prey can be found in Central and South America. It feeds by capturing and picking up monkeys (which weigh up to three times the eagle's body weight) in its claws.

The longest claw of the golden eagle is that of its fourth finger, opposite to the others, which it uses to pierce its victims.

BLACK BEAR—2 IN

WOLF—1.5 IN

The black bear has very robust claws that it uses on long runs (at up to 25 miles per hour!) and to quickly climb up trees.

The large, tough claws of the wolf allow it to walk fast for hours on uneven, muddy, or snow-covered terrain.

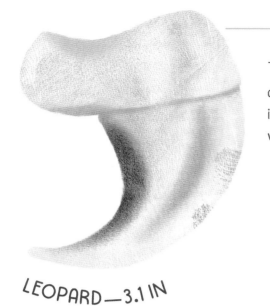

The claws of the leopard are very robust and allow it to climb trees even while holding large prey.

LEOPARD—3.1 IN

The long claws of the snapping turtle are very sharp and can do a lot of damage.

SNAPPING TURTLE—1.5 IN

BOBCAT—1.2 IN

Using its claws, the bobcat is able to climb trees with great agility. From the branches, it stages a deadly ambush on its prey.

AMERICAN PORCUPINE—1.2 IN

The claws found on the four front toes of the American porcupine allow it to easily climb and defend itself.

AMERICAN BADGER—1.75 IN

Strong and resistant, the American badger's claws allow it to dig holes and form long tunnels.

The fox uses its claws—which are very similar to those of dogs—to dig burrows, mark its territory, and catch small prey.

FOX—0.6 IN

COYOTE—1 IN

The coyote uses its claws to flip porcupines onto their backs so that they cannot use their quills to defend themselves.

STRANGE TEETH

BABIRUSA—GREATER THAN 1 FT

The **babirusa** is
an Asian wild pig.
The male's two upper
canine teeth grow
upside down and
emerge on its head,
similar to horns! These
bizarre tusks do not
seem to be used in any
way by the animal.

TIGER—ALMOST 4 IN

The **tiger** is definitely
the most imposing of the
carnivores! Its canine teeth
are both long and sharp,
and its bite is particularly
powerful thanks to the
strong muscles of its jaws.

MUSK DEER—3 TO 4 IN

The **musk deer** has retained
some of its more primordial
characteristics: The male, for
example, does not possess antlers
but is endowed instead with pointed
canine teeth.

HIPPOPOTAMUS—20 IN

The **hippopotamus** feeds exclusively on plants, preferably aquatic ones, but if it gets irritated, it shows off its huge canine teeth—which makes people understand why it's considered the most dangerous animal in Africa!

The **baboon**, omnivorous and aggressive, has sharp canine teeth that it uses to impress rivals, defend its territory from intruders, and of course, hunt.

BABOON—1.4 IN

WHITE SHARK—2.7 IN

The **white shark** has up to seven rows of sharp, serrated teeth. If some of its teeth in the first row break while it's biting, they're immediately replaced by those of the second row and so on! The effect is quite impressive—see for yourself by turning the page!

EGGS

OSTRICH—6 IN

The winner of the largest egg is the **ostrich.** Its egg weighs up to 3 pounds—equal to the size of 25 **chicken** eggs. Compared to the size of the mother though, it's actually the smallest egg.

The female of the **kiwi** lays a single egg that is gigantic compared to the size of the adult. It can weigh up to a fifth of the weight of the mother, who, in the days before laying it, cannot even feed anymore.

CHICKEN—ABOUT 2.2 IN

KIWI—ABOUT 4.7 IN

COMMON LOON—3.5 IN

The **common loon** nests on the shore of lakes and ponds. Its eggs hatch after about a month of being in the nest.

GALÁPAGOS TORTOISE—2.4 IN

The **Galápagos tortoise,** the largest species of tortoise, lays 40 to 50 eggs in a hole dug in the sand. The temperature determines whether male or female tortoises are born.

The female **horn shark** lays about 24 eggs that are a bizarre spiral shape and can reach up to 4.7 inches in length.

HORN SHARK—4.7 IN

The **vervain hummingbird** holds the record for the smallest eggs, which are 0.4 inches in length and weigh less than 0.1 ounce.

VERVAIN HUMMINGBIRD—0.4 IN

SONG THRUSH—1.1 IN

The **song thrush** lays dark blue-turquoise eggs with darker stains on them, camouflaging them well in the nest among the leaves of the trees.

The female **ball python** is the only snake that curls up on top of the eggs it lays, raising their temperature to keep them warm.

BALL PYTHON—3.8 IN

SIX-LINED RACERUNNER LIZARD—7 IN

The **six-lined racerunner** is a lizard, characterized by its long tail, which can exceed more than twice the length of its body. As other lizards, in the event of danger, the tail can be cut off and will then regrow.

The tail of the **domestic shorthair cat** is important for its balance and fundamental for its body language. As an example, a tucked away or fluffed out tail indicates that the cat is scared and may attack.

DOMESTIC SHORTHAIR CAT—12 TO 16 IN

CURLY TAILS

*This tail is not life-size and is just to show the shape of the elephant's tail.

ELEPHANT—59 IN

The **elephant**—the largest land mammal—has ivory tusks, a long trunk that is prehensile (used to grasp objects), wide ears, and a long, thick tail that ends with a tuft of stiff hairs like wire.

TUFTED GROUND SQUIRREL— ABOUT 1 FT

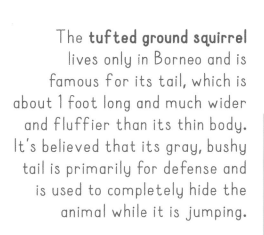

*This squirrel is not life-size.

The **tufted ground squirrel** lives only in Borneo and is famous for its tail, which is about 1 foot long and much wider and fluffier than its thin body. It's believed that its gray, bushy tail is primarily for defense and is used to completely hide the animal while it is jumping.

FOLLOW THE TRACKS

Use the black footprints on this page (which are not to scale) to find the life-size footprints in the dirt.

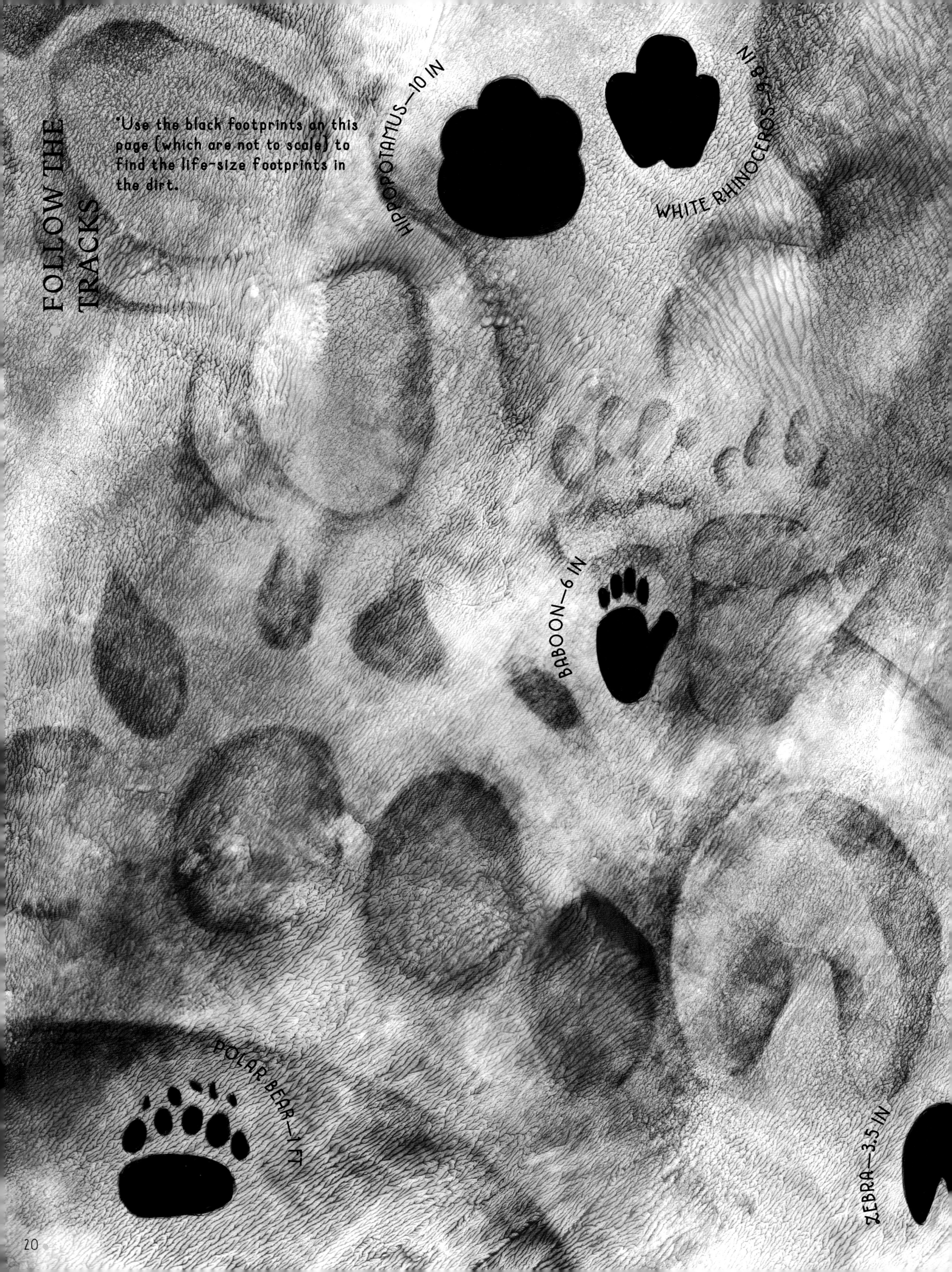

HIPPOPOTAMUS—10 IN

WHITE RHINOCEROS—9.8 IN

BABOON—6 IN

POLAR BEAR—1 FT

ZEBRA—3.5 IN

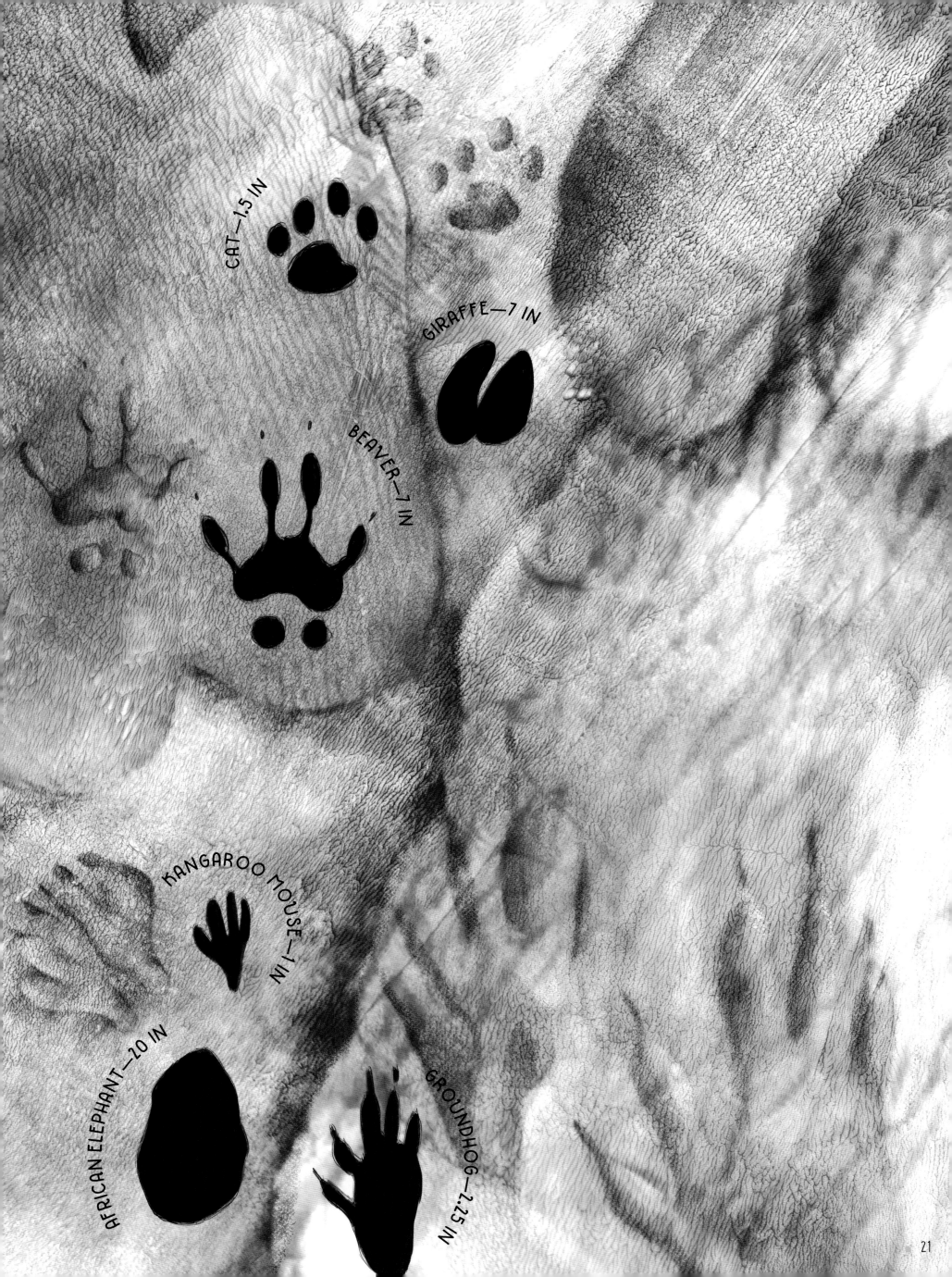

CAT—1.5 IN

GIRAFFE—7 IN

BEAVER—7 IN

KANGAROO MOUSE—1 IN

AFRICAN ELEPHANT—20 IN

GROUNDHOG—2.25 IN

LORDS OF THE NIGHT

At 11 inches in length, the **Australian flying fox** is one of the largest in the bat family. It lives in colonies in Australia and in some tropical Asian areas. Thanks to its incredible wingspan, it can fly for miles in search of flowers and fruits.

AUSTRALIAN FLYING FOX—WINGSPAN 5 FT

BUMBLEBEE BAT—WING SPAN 6 IN

VAMPIRE BAT—WINGSPAN 15 IN

The **vampire bat** lives in South America and feeds on the blood of animals. In spite of its name and its somewhat disturbing eating habits, it is only 3.5 inches long!

GREATER NOCTULE BAT—WINGSPAN UP TO 16 IN

The **greater noctule bat**, whose body measures about 3 inches long, is the largest of the European family of bats.

The **bumblebee bat**, the smallest bat in the world, lives in Asia. It measures just over 1 inch in length and weighs around 0.07 ounces. It feeds on small insects.

23

GOLIATH BEETLES—4.7 IN

It's said that the **ladybug** brings good luck, maybe because this cute red insect is the predator of a large number of plant pests and therefore is a great ally to those who grow flower or vegetable gardens.

LADYBUG—0.4 IN

The **goliath beetle** is the largest of the coleopteran order, the most common insect order with the largest number of existing species. It can weigh up to 2 ounces, which is pretty heavy for an insect!

SMALL GIANTS

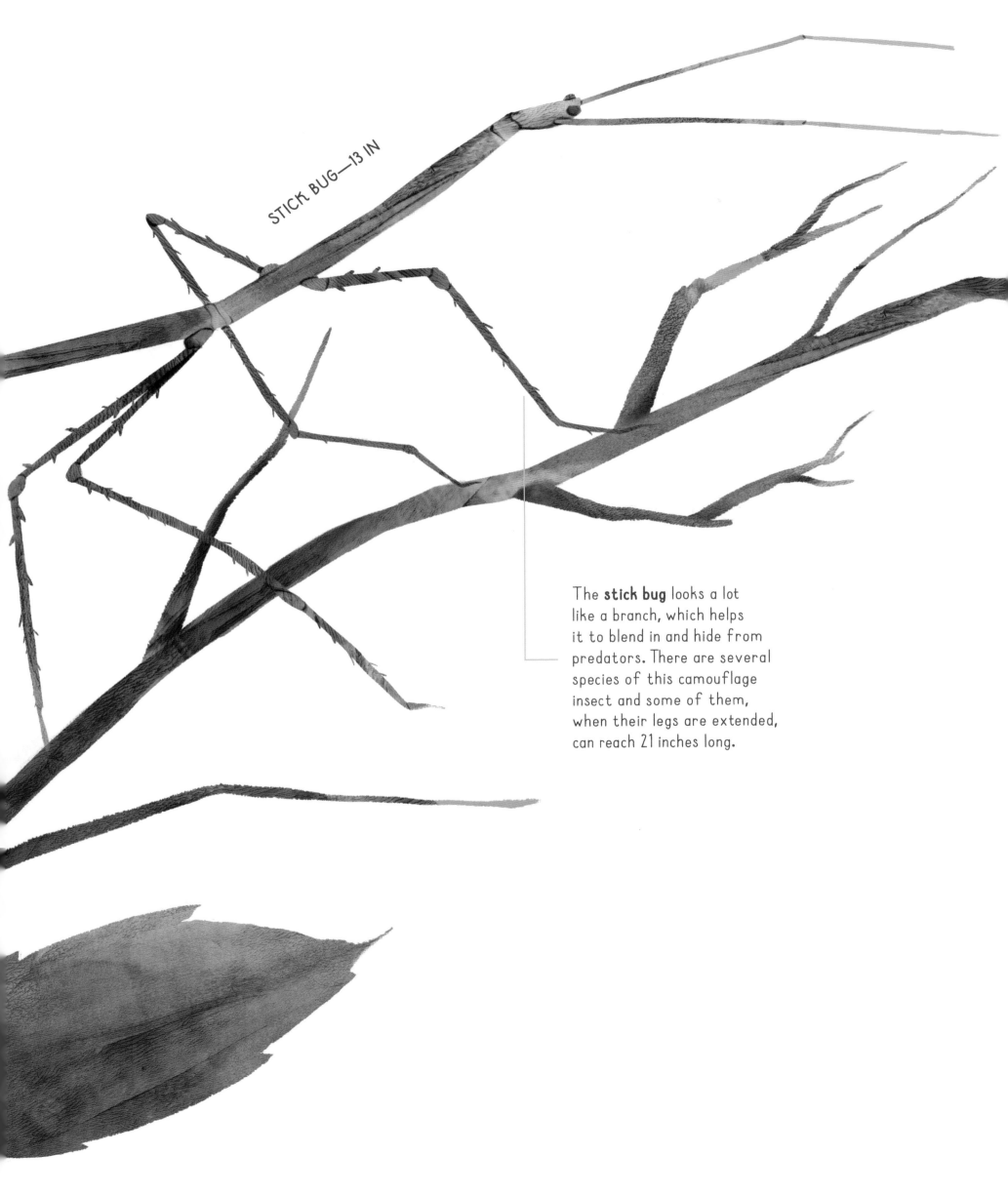

STICK BUG—13 IN

The **stick bug** looks a lot like a branch, which helps it to blend in and hide from predators. There are several species of this camouflage insect and some of them, when their legs are extended, can reach 21 inches long.

RECORD-BREAKING MOTHS AND BUTTERFLIES

QUEEN ALEXANDRA'S BIRDWING BUTTERFLY
WINGSPAN 11 IN/WING HEIGHT 7 IN

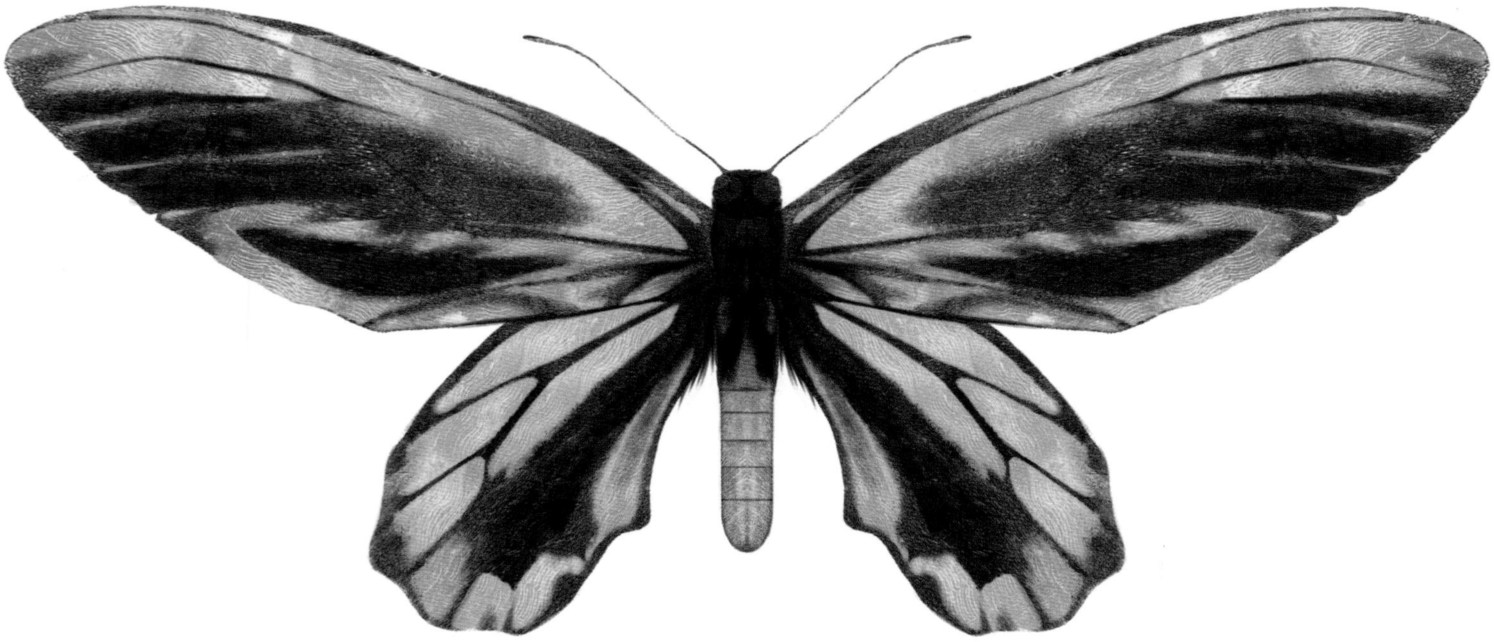

The male of the **Queen Alexandra's birdwing butterfly** species, shown here, is smaller than the female, whose 11-inch wingspan makes it the largest butterfly in the world. It lives in Papua New Guinea and is in grave danger of extinction.

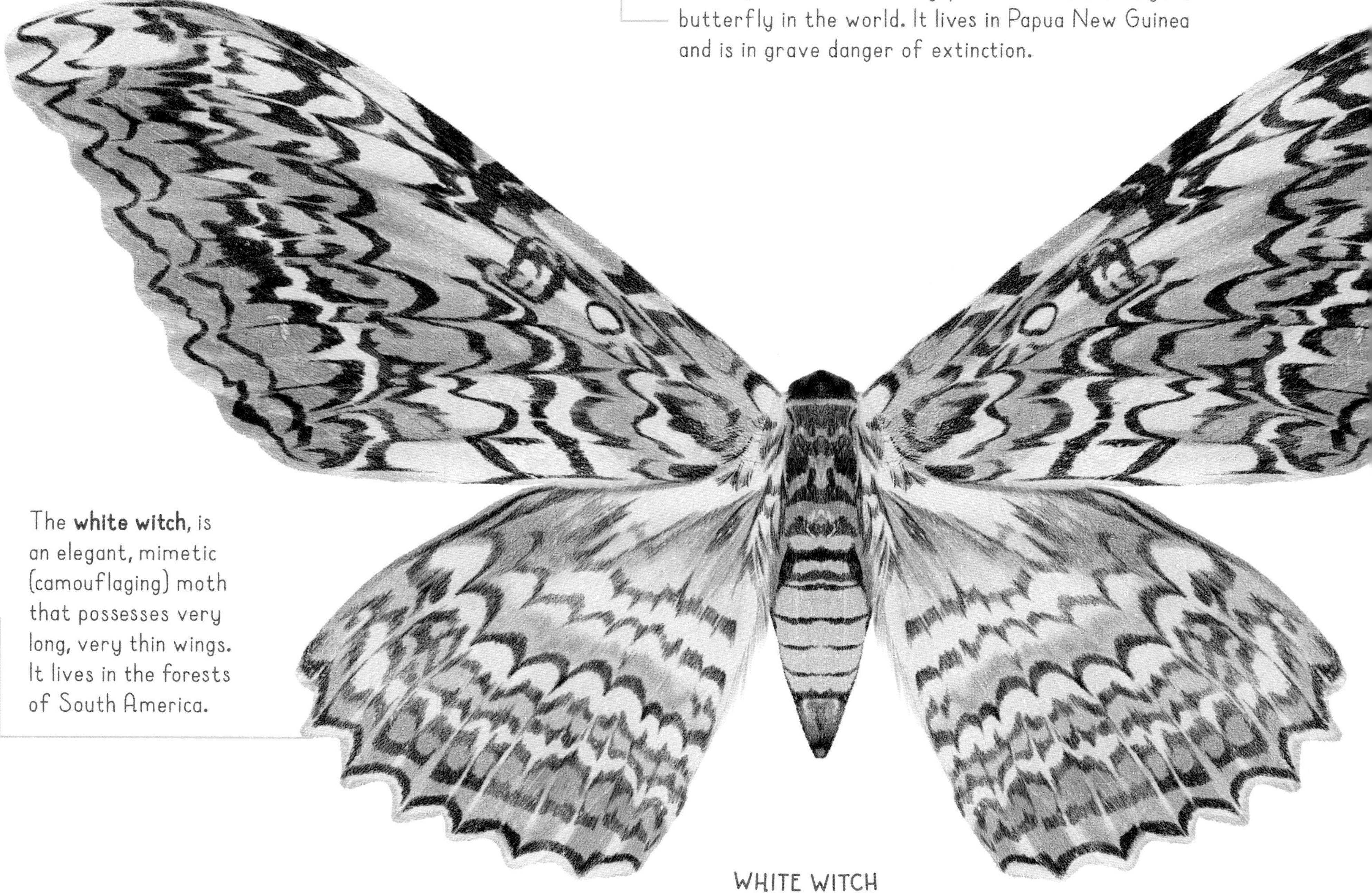

The **white witch**, is an elegant, mimetic (camouflaging) moth that possesses very long, very thin wings. It lives in the forests of South America.

WHITE WITCH
WINGSPAN 1 FT/WING HEIGHT 6 IN

The **Atlas moth** is one of the largest moths in the world. The adult lives for a few days, during which the female can lay as many as 200 eggs at a time.

ATLAS MOTH
WINGSPAN 1 FT/WING HEIGHT 8.3 IN

HERCULES MOTH
WINGSPAN 10 IN/WING HEIGHT 10.6 IN

The short tail of the female **Hercules moth** cannot compete in beauty with the long one found on the male. Its size makes it a spectacular inhabitant of the forests of Australia and New Guinea.

In 1935, the **cane toad** was introduced to Australia to try to limit the spread of cane beetles. The result was not what was hoped for, and the toad reproduced and became a predator to smaller species of toads, thanks to the powerful poison produced by the glands positioned on the sides of its head.

CANE TOAD—9.5 IN

The **spadefoot toad** is a strange toad with vertical pupils that spends most of its time buried in the sand. Its tadpole is very large and can reach up to 6 inches— that's bigger than the adult, which reaches a maximum of 3.5 inches!

0.3 IN

The *Paedophryne amauensis* is the smallest vertebrate in the world. The miniature little toads hatch directly from the eggs and are never tadpoles!

SPADEFOOT TOAD—UP TO 3.5 IN

COMMON EUROPEAN TOAD—UP TO 6 IN

Female **common European toads**
can reach up to 6 inches in
length and are the largest toads
in Europe. They can lay up to
4,000 eggs which hatch into
black tadpoles.

GOLIATH FROG—1 FT

The **goliath frog** lives in Africa. It is the largest frog
in the world and can weigh more than 7.2 pounds.
The male does not have vocal sacs, which serve
to amplify its croaking. It is in danger of extinction.

The **goliath birdeater tarantula** lives in South America. It is one of the largest spiders, but with its 6-ounce weight, it definitely holds the record for being the heaviest. Its poisonous bite is not lethal, but its body's stinging hairs can be very dangerous, especially if inhaled.

GOLIATH BIRDEATER TARATULA—11 IN

PEACOCK SPIDER—0.2 IN

The **peacock spider**, a small Australian jumping spider, is famous for its mating dance, during which the male raises his abdomen and legs to wave at the female.

BLACK WIDOW—2 IN

The **black widow** is an American spider with sedentary habits: It usually waits for its victims to fall into the web woven near its den. The poison that it injects with its bite dissolves its prey and can be lethal to humans!

IN MINIATURE

The **Etruscan pygmy shrew,** which hardly reaches 2 inches long (including its tail), weighs just under 0.1 ounce and is the smallest mammal, next to the bumblebee bat. The Etruscan pygmy shrew is a dangerous predator of spiders and insects: to keep its body temperature constant, it must eat at least its weight in insects. When prey is scarce, or in colder periods of the year, it stiffens and enters into a lethargic state for several hours more than once a day.

ETRUSCAN PYGMY SHREW—2 IN

BIGEYE THRESHER SHARK—DIAMETER ABOUT 4 IN

The **shark**'s eyes are able to reflect the small amount of light available on the sea floor, so it can see even in the darkest waters.

The **tarsier**, a small nocturnal primate, has huge eyes that are fixed in their sockets. To overcome the limitations imposed by this feature, it can rotate its head more than 180 degrees.

EAGLE—DIAMETER 0.7 IN

The **eagle**'s eyes are endowed with a large number of visual cells giving it vision that is 5 times more acute than human vision.

The **rattlesnake** can capture warm-blooded prey at night because its eyes see in infrared.

RATTLESNAKE—DIAMETER 0.3 IN

TARSIER—DIAMETER 0.6 IN

The **giant squid** has the largest eyes of any living animal! They are up to 10 inches in diameter. The squid's eyes are so large to allow it to perceive the faint light of the sea depths and the bioluminescence of the inhabitants of the abyss.

GIANT SQUID—DIAMETER 10 IN

The **blue whale**, which is 75 to 100 feet long, is the largest animal that has ever existed. However, in order to withstand the high pressures of the ocean depths, its pupils measure only 5.9 inches in diameter, as you can see on the next spread.

36–37

ISABELLA GROTT is an illustrator from Rovereto, Italy. She holds degrees from the Art Institute of Trento, the Academy of Fine Arts in Pictorial Decoration, and the Nemo Academy of Digital Arts. She currently lives in Florence with her cat, Miss Murple, and works as a freelance illustrator and teacher at Nemo Academy.

RITA MABEL SCHIAVO is the author of several children's books. She has a degree in Biological Sciences with a naturalistic background from the University of Milan and later deepened her studies especially in herpetology and the field of eco-ethology. She is one of the founding members and administrators of Associazione Didattica Museale (ADM) and ADMaiora, which teach at and choose books for museums, nature parks, oases, and exhibitions. She lives in Italy.

The art for this book was created digitally.

Cataloging-in-Publication Data has been applied for and may be obtained from the Library of Congress.

ISBN 978-1-4197-4460-0

Published in 2020 by Abrams Books for Young Readers, an imprint of ABRAMS.

Printed and bound in China
10 9 8 7 6 5 4 3 2 1

Abrams Books for Young Readers are available at special discounts when purchased in quantity for premiums and promotions as well as fundraising or educational use. Special editions can also be created to specification. For details, contact specialsales@abramsbooks.com or the address below.

Abrams® is a registered trademark of Harry N. Abrams, Inc.

ABRAMS The Art of Books
195 Broadway, New York, NY 10007
abramsbooks.com

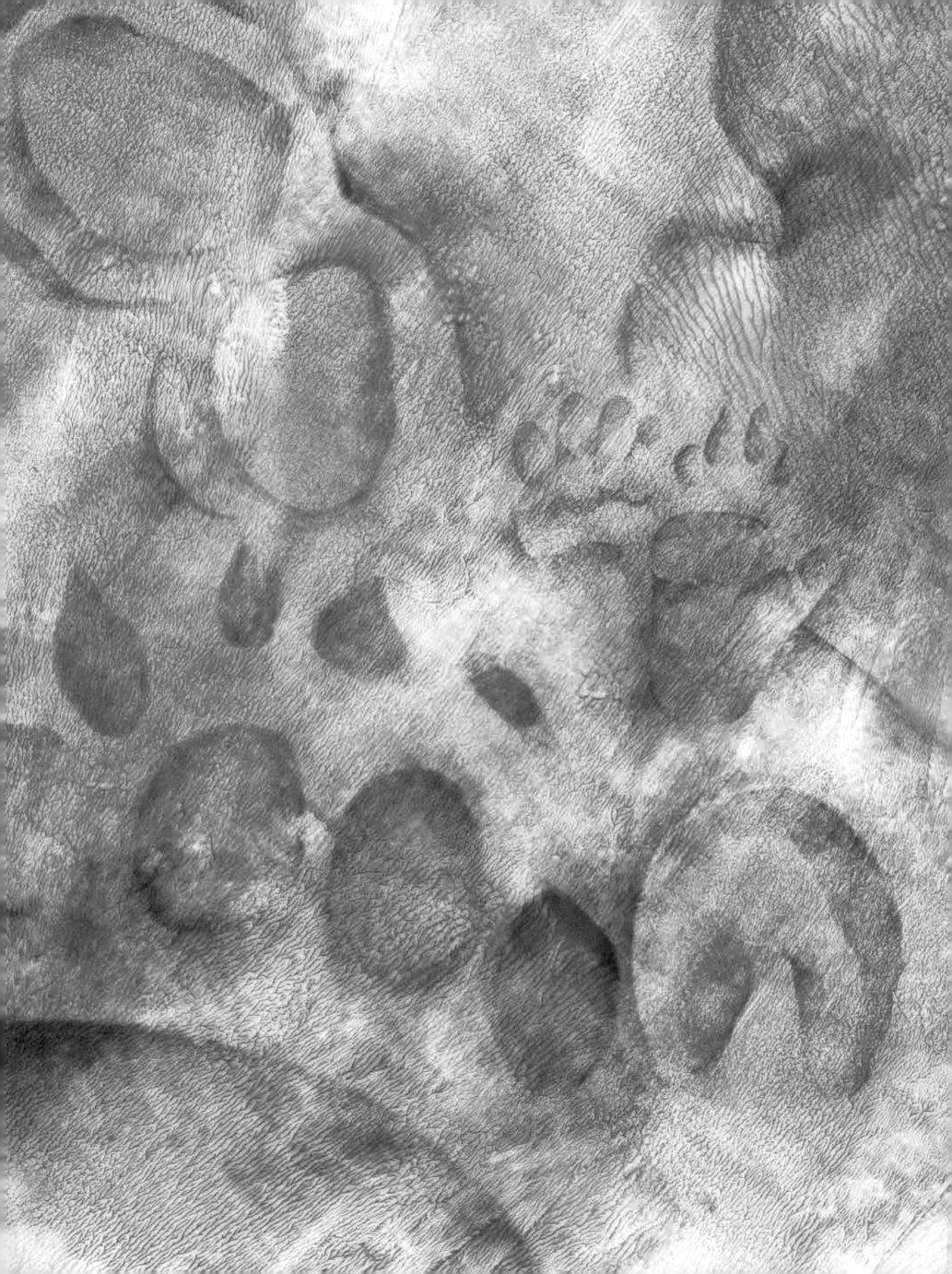

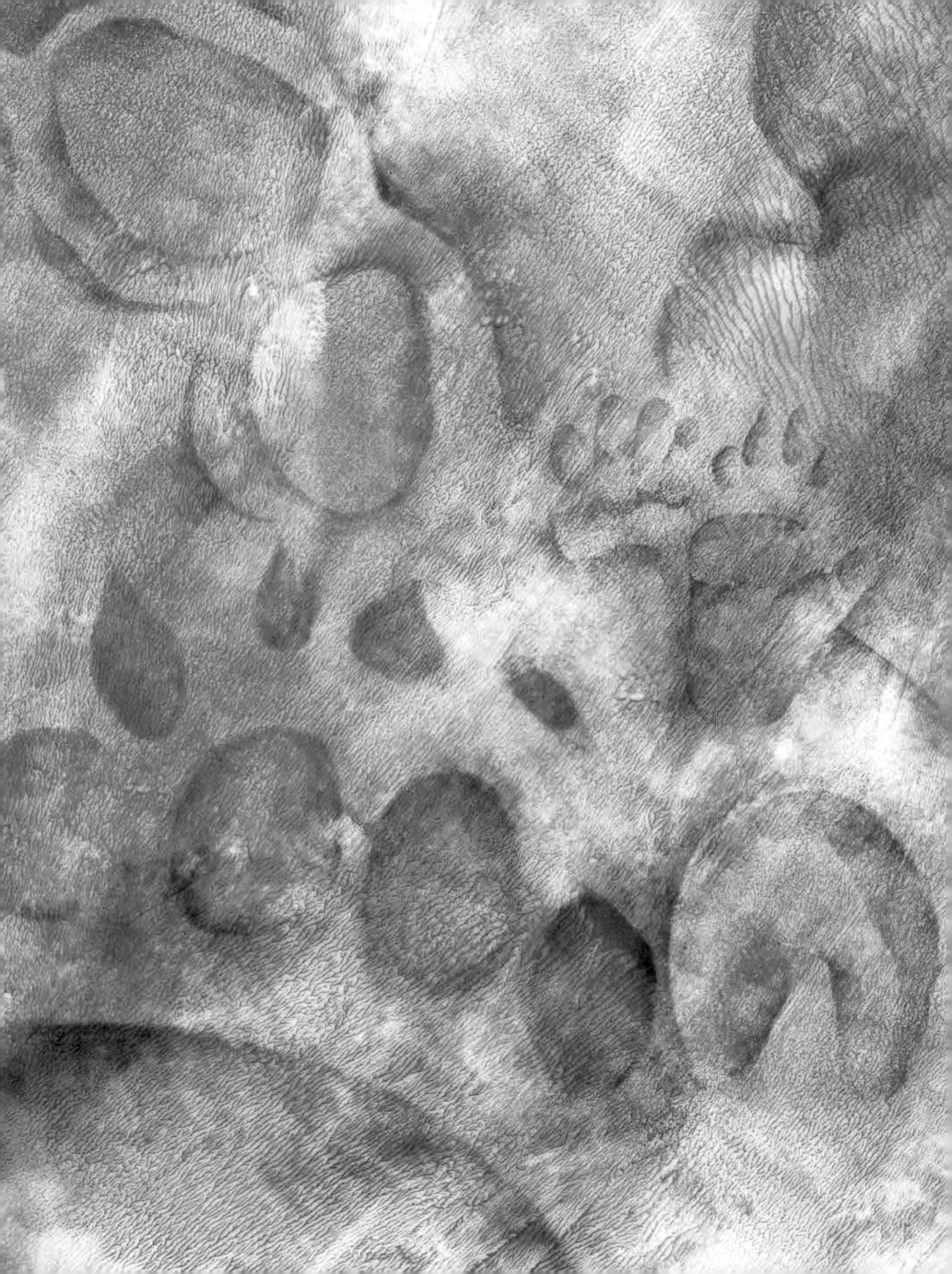